5-26-05

6/05

Tom Brady

Never-Quit Quarterback

Titles in the **SPORTS LEADERS** *Series:*

Tom Brady

Never-Quit Quarterback

Kimberly Gatto

Enslow Publishers, Inc.

40 Industrial Road	PO Box 38
Box 398	Aldershot
Berkeley Heights, NJ 07922	Hants GU12 6BP
USA	UK

http://www.enslow.com

Library of Congress Cataloging-in-Publication Data

Gatto, Kimberly.
    Tom Brady : never-quit quarterback / Kimberly Gatto.— 1st ed.
        p. cm. — (Sports leaders series)
    Includes bibliographical references and index.
    ISBN 0-7660-2475-X
    1. Brady, Tom, 1977– 2. Football players—United States—Biography—
Juvenile literature. I. Title. II. Series.
GV939.B685G38 2005
796.332'092—dc22

                                    2004018494

Printed in the United States of America

10 9 8 7 6 5 4 3 2 1

To Our Readers: We have done our best to make sure all Internet Addresses in this book were active and appropriate when we went to press. However, the author and the publisher have no control over and assume no liability for the material available on those Internet sites or on other Web sites they may link to. Any comments or suggestions can be sent by e-mail to comments@enslow.com or to the address on the back cover.

Illustration Credits: Al Bello/Getty Images, p. 64; Andy Lyons/Allsport, p. 40; Andy Lyons/Getty Images, p. 90; Brad Mangin/MLB Photos via Getty Images, p. 28; Bruce Bennett Studios/Getty Images, p. 19; Darren McCollester/Getty Images, p. 78; Eliot Schechter/Allsport, p. 56; Elsa/Getty Images, p. 72; Ezra Shaw/Getty Images, pp. 6, 10, 14, 61, 76, 80; Focus On Sport/Getty Images, p. 22; Harry How/Allsport, p. 36; Jamie Squire/Allsport, pp. 31, 59; Jeff Gross/Getty Images, p. 85; Jeff Haynes/AFP/Getty Images, p. 88; Jonathan Daniel/Getty Images, p. 70; Rick Stewart/Allsport, p. 48; Tom Hauck/Allsport, p. 42; Tom Pidgeon/Allsport, p. 51.

Cover Illustration: Ezra Shaw/Getty Images.

CONTENTS

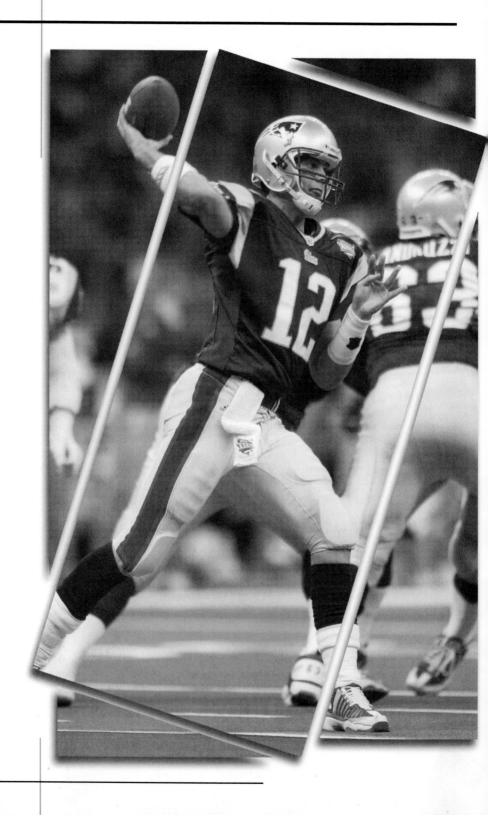

MAKING HISTORY

Red, white, and blue banners soared from the stands at the Louisiana Superdome. Spectators danced in their seats. New England football fans had waited nearly half a century for this moment. At halftime of Super Bowl XXXVI, the New England Patriots led the St. Louis Rams, 14–3. Were the underdog Patriots finally about to make history?

Most experts doubted that the Patriots could hold on to their lead. The team had finished the previous season with a dismal 5–11 record. Although the Patriots had certainly earned their place at the Super Bowl, many believed their new success was a fluke. The team seemed a mismatch for the Rams, the most powerful team in the National Football League (NFL).

Led by superstar quarterback Kurt Warner, the Rams were favored by 14 points. The team boasted the best offense and the leading record in the NFL (14–2). In fact, the Rams had won two Super Bowls in just three years. Sportswriters and fans called the team "the Greatest Show on Turf."

"The only team that can beat us is us," boasted Rams star Marshall Faulk.[1] The media seemed to agree. As one reporter noted, "compared to Kurt Warner and the Rams, the Patriots looked like high schoolers."[2]

At the center of this modern fairytale was the Patriots' quarterback, Tom Brady. A lanky twenty-four-year-old from California, Brady had been a fourth-stringer during the prior year. Days before the Super Bowl, Patriots coach Bill Belichick had chosen Brady to start in place of the team's nine-year veteran, Drew Bledsoe. Brady had led the Patriots to thirteen victories after Bledsoe was injured early in the season. While Bledsoe had been cleared to play, Belichick placed his faith in Brady.

Many wondered whether Belichick had made the right choice. Brady was a relative newcomer, while Bledsoe had played in three Pro Bowls. At 6'4" and

220 pounds, Brady was much lighter than the other quarterbacks. He was not a quick runner, nor could he throw particularly deep. Furthermore, Brady had sprained his left ankle during the prior week's AFC Championship. His foot remained painful and swollen.

Despite all these questions, Coach Belichick stuck to his decision. In his opinion, Brady had jumped in when it mattered and had never let the team down. What the young quarterback lacked in raw talent, he made up for with his confidence and his toughness. He worked harder than any other player, and his teammates respected him. As

> **Brady had jumped in when it mattered and had never let the team down.**

the coach saw it, Brady's leadership had brought the Patriots this far.

Together with Coach Belichick, the team developed a game plan that would emphasize their strengths. Veteran Adam Vinatieri was one of league's best clutch kickers. Defensive backs Lawyer Milloy, Ty Law, and Otis Smith were playing especially well. The Patriots could tackle hard and were not afraid to do so. Overall, the Patriots felt that they were a more physical team than the Rams. Their

Tom Brady attempts to run for a first down during Superbowl XXXVI at the Superdome in New Orleans on February 3, 2002.

plan was to disrupt the Rams' timing and, at the same time, tire the superstars out.

In order to achieve this goal, the Patriots decided to emphasize their unity as a team. They felt that this would solidify them in the eyes of their opponents. Traditionally, each starter was introduced to the crowd separately. The Patriots, however, chose to begin their own tradition. They would be introduced simply as "the New England Patriots." There would be no stars; starters and benchwarmers would arrive on the field as a team.

"The players wanted to do it that way; they wanted to come out as a team," said Coach Belichick.[3]

This team strategy appeared to be working early in the game. Ty Law caught a misfire by Warner and returned it 47 yards for a touchdown. Brady then spotted David Patten in the back end zone. The quarterback threw an 8-yard pass to Patten to bring the Patriots up by eleven points.

"A huge throw," Patten said after the game. "Because we didn't want to settle for a field goal there, and because it shook [the Rams] up being behind by that much at halftime." Brady "put the ball right where it had to be."[4]

Tom Brady was not the only one playing well. The Patriots tackled Warner, Isaac Bruce, Marshall Faulk, and the other Rams stars again and again. Warner aggravated an old injury to the thumb on his throwing hand. Faulk began to appear worn and battered. By the beginning of the third quarter, the Rams seemed less intimidating. Nevertheless, defeating the Rams—tired or not—would not be an easy feat.

Adam Vinatieri was ready to take that chance. The kicker made a field goal in the third quarter, increasing the Patriots' lead to 17–3. Then the Rams came back with a vengeance. Warner moved his team into the end zone in a series of three plays. The star then completed a 26-yard scoring pass to Ricky Proehl for a touchdown along the left sideline. Warner had tied the game at 17–17, with 1:37 left. The Rams' defense held the Patriots down through-out the entire second half of play.

"I thought we were back in the ball game and were going to win this thing," said Proehl. "Momentum had changed."[5]

With 1:21 and no timeouts remaining, New England got the ball on their own 17-yard line.

> "[Brady] put the ball right where it had to be."
> —David Patten

Brady was now faced with a tough decision. Would he be conservative and let the clock wind down, to take this battle into overtime? Or would he take a chance at an immediate victory?

Playing conservatively "wasn't even on my mind," Brady later said. "I was planning to go out there and win the game."[6]

Brady completed 5 of 8 passes for 53 yards. Twice he made spikes to stop the clock. He began his open-ing drive with a 5-yard flare pass to J.R. Redmond, then made a 23-yard pass—his longest of the day—to Troy Brown at the Rams' 36-yard line.

"That was the big play," Brady later said. "It's

called '64 Max All-End,' and the Max stands for, as my coach says, 'We need the maximum time for me to throw.'"[7]

A 6-yard hit to tight-end Jermaine Wiggins moved the ball to the Rams' 30. Displaying the skill of a veteran player, Brady moved his team into field goal range. The crowd gasped. There were 0:07 seconds remaining on the clock.

Brady sprinted off the field. Kicker Adam Vinatieri had been waiting for Brady's call, and was ready and willing to answer. As the final seconds wore down, Vinatieri completed a 48-yard field goal, for a final score of 20–17. The red, white, and blue–shirted crowd went wild. The underdog Patriots had won the Super Bowl.

Reporters and fans were shocked by the win. News reporters proclaimed the win "one of the greatest upsets in Super Bowl history." The glorious Rams had been defeated. But Coach Belichick and the Patriots were not completely surprised.

"Tom's done it several times for us under pressure," Belichick later said. "[He] did a super job of managing the game."[8]

Brady's teammate David Patten added, "You can't say enough about that kid. He has a tremendous amount of confidence; he has led this team."[9]

*Tom Brady celebrates on the field of the Superdome after help-
ing lead the New England Patriots to an upset victory in Super
Bowl XXXVI against the heavily favored St. Louis Rams.*

With 16 completions on 27 attempts, for 145
yards and one touchdown, Tom Brady was named
Most Valuable Player (MVP). At 24, he became
the youngest quarterback in Super Bowl history to
earn that honor. Overall, Brady became the third
youngest MVP in history. Only the legendary
Marcus Allen and Lynn Swann had been younger.

Brady had wise words for his many young fans.
"Don't let other people tell you what you're capable
of," he said. "As long as you believe in yourself and

work hard to achieve whatever you set your mind to, you just keep plugging away."[10]

Brady had always been known for his good sportsmanship. This time would be no different. When asked how he felt about being named MVP, Brady quickly credited his teammates.

"I think our whole team is MVP," Brady said. "We have an MVT—a Most Valuable Team."[11]

2

EARLY YEARS

Thomas Edward Brady, Jr., was born on August 3, 1977, to Thomas and Galynn (Johnson) Brady. Tom Sr. worked in the insurance business, while Galynn, a former airline stewardess, stayed at home to care for the children. Tom and his older sisters, Maureen, Julie, and Nancy, were raised in San Mateo, California, just south of San Francisco.

The Bradys were a close-knit family who enjoyed spending time together. They particularly liked sports. Maureen and Nancy excelled at softball, Julie was a top soccer player, and Tom was a budding baseball star. As a result, the family schedule was jam-packed with sporting events. Tom Sr. and Galynn posted the kids' sporting events on a huge calendar in the family kitchen. One year, the calendar included 300 events.

While baseball was young Tom's primary sport, he also had a strong passion for football. For many years, the Brady family held season tickets to the San Francisco 49ers games, which took place at nearby Candlestick Park. "Every Sunday, we'd head out, when they were in town," Tom said. "We'd tailgate. Until we started getting older and we had sports on the weekend, it was really something fun for our family to do."[1]

One of Tom's earliest memories was attending the 1981 NFC Championship game between the 49ers and the superstar Dallas Cowboys. Four-year-old Tom spent the entire first half crying because he wanted a souvenir. "I was crying to my Dad because he wouldn't buy me one of those big Nerf #1 fingers," Tom remembered. "Finally, at the end of the first half . . . he gave me [one] and it kind of kept me quiet for the rest of the game."[2]

That game turned out to include one of the greatest moments in NFL history. It would be forever referred to as "The Catch," because near the end of the last quarter, Dwight Clark miraculously caught Joe Montana's pass in the end zone to win the game, 28–27. The crowd of 60,000 erupted in the stands.

"I remember everyone standing up . . . my parents too," Tom said. "Everyone stood up and I couldn't see anything. I had my Dad kind of lift me up. He said, 'The 49ers won! The 49ers won!'"[3]

It was a huge victory for San Francisco, who advanced to their first Super Bowl. Led by Joe Montana, the team would go on to win four Super Bowl titles within the next nine years. The 49ers became known as "The Team of the Decade."

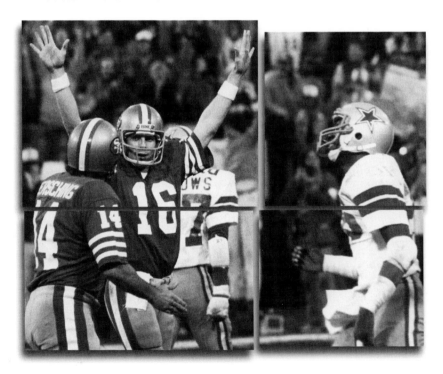

Legendary quarterback Joe Montana (16) of the San Francisco 49ers celebrates his team's victory over the Dallas Cowboys in the 1981 NFC Championship Game. A four-year-old Tom Brady was among those fans who attended the game at San Francisco's Candlestick Park.

Tom was mesmerized by Joe Montana's brilliant plays, and dreamed of one day becoming a star quarterback himself. One of Tom's favorite shirts was a red Joe Montana "Number 16" jersey. "He'd wear that [jersey] all the time," explained Tom Sr. "As a family we were kind of nuts into this stuff, so we would go to the game and then even come home at night and watch the game on replay."[4]

"He [Montana] was the guy I looked up to," Tom later said. "And still idolize."[5]

> "He [Montana] was the guy I looked up to. . . And still idolize."
>
> —Tom Brady

Since there were no organized youth football leagues in the San Mateo area, Tom and his school friends held their own games during recess. "You'd already have your team picked before you went out for recess," Tom recalled. "So you didn't waste any time out there. It was football. It was football in the schoolyard. It was football when I'd get home from school. And, of course, always watching it on TV."[6]

After school and on weekends, the games extended into the neighborhood as well. "Football back in the day was like, you'd gather up all your friends," Tom later recalled. "The two best players always got to be the captains. Then you'd flip a coin for who had the first pick. Then once you'd get your team, you would play for hours."[7]

Tom's cousin, Paul Johnson, remembered: "Whether it was a football or baseball, Tom was always throwing a ball around."[8]

Tom's work ethic was spurred by his strong competitive drive. Even as a young child, he hated to lose at anything. Tom would often challenge his sisters to video or card games, and would keep playing until he won. "Every time I'd lose," Tom later said, "I'd just throw a fit."[9]

It was this competitive nature that drove Tom to excel. He had to work hard, because unlike most athletes, he was not particularly quick or strong. In fact, Tom's friends were better football players than he was. "Tommy was always the underdog," said Bobby Paul, one of Tom's childhood friends.[10] But Tom always loved a challenge. At one point, he chose the fastest runner in the neighborhood and challenged him to repeated races around the block. Each time he lost, Tom would vow to improve.

"I just kept challenging him until I beat him," Tom later said. "It's like the tortoise and the hare. I was the tortoise."[11]

"He was a determined kid," said Tom's grandfather, Gordon Johnson. "Whatever he did, he wanted to do

Joe Montana was Tom Brady's football role model. Montana's No. 16 jersey was Brady's favorite shirt to wear.

it right. He was just one of those guys that wouldn't give up."[12]

Tom Brady Sr. saw a glimpse into his son's football future when Tom was twelve years old. On a family vacation in Mexico, Tom bet his dad that he could throw a football through a tire nearly twenty yards away. Tom threw the ball through the tire, not just once, but several times in a row. Tom Sr. was stunned. "I just paused and said, 'My God, where did that ever come from?'" he later said. "I had never seen him throw a football, other than in the street."[13]

Tom himself was not surprised. He knew that if he set his mind to something and kept working hard at it, he could become a great football player. It would not be an easy road, but Tom was willing to give it his all.

3

YOUNG ALL-STAR

T om Brady entered Junipero Serra High School in 1991 with high hopes for the future. Serra, an all-boys Catholic school, was known for its strong academic and sports programs. Several top athletes had graduated from Serra, including football Hall of Famer Lynn Swann and baseball superstar Barry Bonds.

Tom instantly fit into Serra's baseball program, which was one of the strongest in the area. "[Tom Brady] was one of our best players as a catcher, a left-handed hitter," said Pete Jensen, Serra's baseball coach. "He's one of the greatest kids I ever coached. He was a really competitive kid but he kept things in perspective. He loved practice and being on the field; he took extra time in the batting cage and wanted to be as good as he could. He was probably the best catcher I've ever coached."[1]

In addition to baseball, Tom was able to play organized football for the first time in his life. He began as a backup quarterback on Serra's all-freshman team, with hopes of one day moving up to junior varsity. Tom was both excited and nervous.

"I always had nerves because I didn't know the game that well, and I wasn't that confident in football and my skills," Tom recalled. "I didn't even know how to put the pads in the pants. I didn't know how to put anything on. All I knew how to do was throw the ball."[2]

The freshman team finished the season without a win. Tom worked hard over the summer months to learn the "ins and outs" of organized football, and in the fall earned a spot on the junior varsity team. When the starting quarterback decided to give up football for another sport, Tom received more playing time. The team finished with a slightly better record that year.

But "slightly better" was not enough for Tom Brady. He was determined to play varsity in his junior year, and was willing to work harder to do so.

After reviewing his game, Tom decided that he needed to improve his footwork and build up his physical stamina. Rather than spending his free time hanging out with friends, Tom worked out at the gym and attended training sessions. Tom's fitness regimen included a rigorous jump rope workout that was soon added to the entire team's exercise routine.

Tom "made a tremendous commitment both to himself and to our football program," said Serra's football coach, Tom MacKenzie. "I never had to ask him to do any of these things. These were personal decisions he made on his own because he wanted the opportunity to play on the next level. I never needed to tell Tom Brady that he needed to work hard."[3]

> **"He's one of the greatest kids I ever coached."**
> —Pete Jensen

Tom's hard work paid off, and he made the varsity team. As his body grew stronger, Tom became more confident in his game. "Varsity was my third year, my junior year," he later said. "It was really when I started to really develop the fact that, hey, I could be pretty good at this game."[4]

By his senior year, Tom's skills had improved immensely. In a game against American High School that season, Tom threw three touchdown passes in

Star baseball player Barry Bonds attended Junipero Serra High School, the same high school Tom Brady would enter in 1991. Before committing himself to football, Brady also excelled at baseball.

a row. In another game, he threw two touchdown passes to lead the Serra Padres past their longtime archrival, St. Ignatius. Tom completed his high school career with 236 of 447 passes (52.8%), for 3,702 yards and 31 touchdowns.

"My favorite plays are always when you throw the ball as far as you can downfield," Tom recalled. "We had a play called a Dodge Route. These guys cross and then they just both run up field. We had our two fastest guys out there. So we must have thrown five touchdowns my senior year on that play."[5]

Coach MacKenzie was impressed with Tom's good sportsmanship. "He was always able to keep things in perspective, and fit in both around the school building and around the locker room; he never went out of his way to make himself the center of attention. He was always very conscious that he was just one member of the football team."[6]

Tom earned varsity letters in both football and baseball, and maintained a GPA of 3.5 in his years at Serra. He was named 1994 All-American quarterback by *Blue Chip Illustrated* and *Prep Football Report*, and earned All-State and All-Far West distinctions.

While football was quickly becoming Tom's number-one passion, he continued to excel at baseball.

He completed his high school baseball career with a record of .311 batting, with 8 home runs, 11 doubles, and 44 RBIs. Tom also was named an All-League catcher. One of the highlights of Tom's baseball career was leading Serra to victory over the team's toughest opponents, the San Jose Bellarmine Prep "Bells." Tom hit two home runs that day to clinch the win for Serra.

Tom's baseball talent was spotted by a number of professional scouts; often, 10 or more were in attendance at his games. The Montreal Expos had their sights on Tom, and recruited him in the 18th round of the 1995 amateur draft. It is likely that Tom would have been chosen earlier in the draft, but he had made it clear that college football—not pro baseball—was his goal.

The Expos invited Tom to work out with them as they prepared for a game at Candlestick Park. While Tom enjoyed working out with the pro players, he turned down the Expos' employment offer. Tom Brady was determined to become a pro quarterback.

"I loved them both [baseball and football]," he recalled. "I loved baseball for certain reasons. I played baseball my whole career growing up, my whole life; and then football was like really new, and it was cool, and it was fun."[7]

Tom Brady had many options available to him upon graduating high school—including professional baseball. Ultimately, he chose to play college football at Michigan.

Tom's athletic achievements and excellent grades earned the attention of many colleges. He was offered a football scholarship to the University of California, with the chance to start in the quarterback position. Tom also received a scholarship offer from the University of Michigan, which was known for its competitive football program—so competitive, in fact, that there were six quarterbacks in line for the starting job. Tom's chances of starting—or even playing—at Michigan would be slim.

"Cal [the University of California] told him that he could start as a sophomore, junior and senior, and Michigan said, `We already have six quarterbacks,'" Tom Sr. remembered.[8]

Tom chose the more challenging option, and enrolled at Michigan.

4

MICHIGAN DAYS

The Michigan Wolverines regularly played before a sellout crowd of 112,000 screaming fans. The team, headed by coach Lloyd Carr, was known for its strong defensive line. Carr, who took over in 1995 after 15 years as assistant coach, demanded excellence from his team.

The Wolverines' starting quarterback position was shared by two outstanding players, freshman Scott Dreisbach and sophomore Brian Griese. With such superstars on the Wolverines' roster, there appeared to be little room for Brady. In his first season, Brady was "red-shirted," which meant that he could practice and work out with the team, but could not play. That way, he would not lose a year of eligibility. Brady would need to impress Coach Carr in order to earn a starting position.

Brady worked hard in the off-season and, in 1996, was named third-string quarterback behind Dreisbach and Griese. He played in only two games that season, completing 3 of 5 passes for 26 yards. Brady, who was used to spending his time on the field rather than the bench, began to wonder if he had made the right decision in attending Michigan. He considered transferring to the University of California.

"At the time, Dreisbach was the starter, Griese was the backup and Tom was third string," Lloyd Carr remembered. "He started to think about transferring because Griese had two years of eligibility left and the other guy had three. I told him that he was probably being premature about it, but that he should talk to his dad and then come back to me. He came back the next morning and said, 'Coach, I'm going to prove to you that I'm the best quarterback you have, and I'm going to stay here.'"[1]

Proving himself was nothing new to Brady. He believed in himself, and knew that with hard work, he could outplay the other starters. Brady spent his free time studying game films and working out at the gym. He watched the other players, learning from both their successes and failures. By the time the 1997 preseason rolled around, this extra work had begun to pay off. Brady's passes in training camp impressed Coach Carr and the entire team.

Brady earned some well-deserved playing time at the start of that season. In October, however, he underwent an emergency appendectomy and did not play for the remainder of the season. As Brady watched from the bench, the Wolverines had a stellar year, thanks in part to the team's great defense. Undefeated in the regular season, the team went on to win the Rose Bowl, 21–16, over Washington State. Brian Griese was named MVP. The Wolverines then attended their first national championship in 49 years, sharing the title with the University of Nebraska.

> "I'm going to prove to you that I'm the best quarterback you have."
>
> —Tom Brady

The 1998 season marked several changes for the Wolverines. Brian Griese graduated, and was selected in the third round of the NFL draft by the Denver Broncos. Coach Carr began to realize that Scott Dreisbach was not the player he wanted to lead the team. Coming off of a championship season, Coach

Tom Brady fades back to pass during a game against the Purdue Boilermakers at the Michigan Stadium in Ann Arbor, Michigan.

Carr knew that the team would need a stronger leader. Brady was placed in the starting quarterback position.

Michigan fans were unsettled at the prospect of Brady leading the Wolverines. Although they had faith in the powerful Brian Griese, Brady was simply a newcomer to them. It did not help matters when the team lost their first two games of the season, to Notre Dame and Syracuse.

Brady decided to meet with his teammates in an effort to boost morale. He felt that the players needed to work together better, and to trust him as their quarterback. Brady also oversaw the team's workouts. This plan seemed to work. With Brady leading the team, the Wolverines won eight of their next nine games. The team tied for the Big 10 Conference championship, and won a bid to play Arkansas in the Florida Citrus Bowl. It was a tough game from the start, and by the fourth quarter, Michigan was trailing, 31–24.

But Brady was not about to lose this game. After having two passes intercepted, he engineered two drives in the final quarter to lead the Wolverines to a 45–31 victory. "We wanted to finish the season strong after the disappointing start we had," said Coach Carr. "This team had a disadvantage in that they were always going to be compared to the [1997] national championship team."[2]

Brady did not mind the comparison. He played extremely well that season, completing 214 of 350 passes (61.1%) for 2,636 yards and 15 touchdowns. Only one player, Jim Harbaugh, had ever thrown for more yards in a season for the Wolverines. Brady was named an Academic All-Big 10 Pick and an All-Big 10 Conference honorable mention. He also set a Michigan record for the most attempts (350) and completions (214) in one season.

The 1999 season, however, brought increased competition for Brady. Drew Henson, whom sportswriters described as "the best athlete ever recruited" by Michigan, joined the Wolverines. Suddenly, Brady found himself sharing time with the younger quarterback. Dhani Jones, Brady's teammate at Michigan, remembered, "The hype was all for Henson, not so much with Brady."[3]

This new rivalry with Henson boosted Brady's competitive drive. "Every throw was important in practice," Brady later said.

> We used to split reps 50–50. We'd be counting: "I got eight throws. He got eight throws. What were the stats?" It was fierce, fierce competition, and it was always to the point where you'd wait for game day so you could get out there and compete

against a different team. A lot of times, dealing with that Wednesday night or Thursday night practice where you didn't play well helps you develop that mental toughness, develop some thick skin and realize that you've got to continue to go out there and compete and improve.[4]

With two outstanding quarterbacks on the roster, Coach Carr was in a difficult situation. Carr could not imagine keeping either Brady or Henson on the bench, so he rotated the two players as starters throughout the early season. When the crucial "Big Ten" games of the season arrived, fans wondered who would be named the starter. Ultimately, the decision to start Brady, rather than Henson, came down to three traits: "Consistency. Confidence. Decision making," according to Stan Parrish, Michigan's quarterback coach at the time. "It was in the best interests of the team."[5]

Brady proved that he was worthy of the honor. He led the Wolverines to a 10–2 season, including a win over Ohio State and a chance to face Alabama in the Orange Bowl. Parrish recalled, "We beat Alabama in the Orange Bowl and Brady was spectacular. Nobody worked

> **"You've got to continue to go out there and compete and improve."**
>
> **—Tom Brady**

Brady carries the ball against the Arkansas Razorbacks in the Citrus Bowl on January 1, 1999.

harder to improve himself or to learn more than Tom Brady."[6]

Alabama had taken an early lead in the Orange Bowl, up 14–0 in the first half. Brady then drove the team 44 yards, including a 27-yard strike with 58 seconds left in the half. The game eventually went into overtime, where Michigan scored a 35–34 victory. Brady's performance, which included 33 of 45 passing for 344 yards and 3 touchdowns, earned him game MVP honors.

"That [Orange Bowl] was certainly an outstanding performance," Carr recalled. "But my favorite that season was the one at Penn State—down by 10 points, with six minutes to go, Brady had thrown an interception that went back for a touchdown, and he takes us back on two incredible drives [for touchdown passes] where any mistake by a quarterback would have ended it."[7]

Brady accomplished a great deal during his years at Michigan. He ranked second overall (behind Elvis Grbac) for the most touchdown passes (20) by a Wolverines quarterback in a single season. He earned three letters at Michigan and went 20–5 as a two-year starter. Brady ranked third in Michigan history in attempts (710) and completions (442), fourth in

Brady is set to launch a pass against Notre Dame during a game played in Michigan on September 4, 1999.

yards (5,351) and completion percentage (62.3%), and fifth in touchdown passes (35).

Despite such accomplishments, Brady remained as humble and down-to-earth as he'd always been. Billy Harris, a coach from Michigan State, was impressed by Brady's generosity towards his young fans. "The one memory that I'll always have about [Tom Brady] would be when we came back and got a chance to see him play the last game against Ohio State," said Harris. "Seeing him out there in front of Crisler Arena when everybody else was gone, he had all these little kids around him and asking for his autograph. And there's Tom, just standing like the average guy, sitting around there saying 'I'm going to stay here until they're all gone because I know that if I was a little kid and I was trying to get an auto-graph, I'd hope that they'd stick around and give it to me.'"[8]

5

PRO PLAYER

Tom Brady graduated from Michigan with a degree in organizational studies. He was now ready to join the ranks of the NFL. Yet despite his success as a college quarterback, Brady was not touted as a top draft pick. The problem was his physical stature. At 6'4", Brady weighed a mere 195 pounds. Reporters at *Pro Football Weekly* commented on Brady's lanky physique, describing him as "very skinny," "frail," and "narrow."[1]

In addition, some NFL scouts mistakenly thought that Brady had been an understudy to Drew Henson. "The young kid [Henson] looked like the better quarterback," said one NFL executive. "He had a stronger arm and he could run better."[2] Brady was perceived as backup material, while Henson was viewed as a top-rate starter.

These criticisms upset Brady. The way he saw it, his size should not be a deciding factor. He was a great team leader. And he knew how to win football games—he had proven it at Michigan. Brady had faith that the NFL executives would see him for what he really was—a top-notch quarterback.

> He [Brady] was a great team leader. And he knew how to win football games.

Brady watched the NFL draft with his family in the living room of the Brady family home. Time ticked away. Five rounds of players were selected, but Brady was not among them. As each player was chosen, Brady became more frustrated. At one point, he got up, grabbed a baseball bat, and went into the backyard of his family home to "blow off some steam." He could not understand why no team had chosen him. In Brady's own words, he was "heartbroken."[3]

One team, however, saw something special in Tom Brady. The New England Patriots, headed by Coach Bill Belichick, had a hunch that Brady could become a top NFL player. The Patriots were in search of another backup for their superstar quarterback, Drew Bledsoe. The team's existing backups, Michael Bishop and John Friesz, did not have the strength that Belichick wanted. Young Bishop was not progressing quickly enough, and Friesz was nearing the end of his career. Belichick and his staff viewed Brady as a potential low-risk, late-round pick. Brady was chosen as the 199th pick overall, in the sixth round of the two-day draft.

Brady was grateful to have been chosen by the Patriots.

> You're always kind of hoping you're one of the top guys. It just didn't work out. I think some people just didn't think I possessed the qualities to be a quarterback in the NFL because I slipped down behind a bunch of players. It was a long first day [of the draft]. I really didn't anticipate getting picked on the first day, anyway. Then the second day, that got to be a really long day. The middle of the sixth round, I'm thinking, "I might not get picked. I mean, what am I going to do?" After that, finally getting picked was just a relief. It's really been a period since then of just trying to improve.[4]

Brady was ready to prove to everyone that he was, in fact, worthy of an NFL starting position. As he had in years past, Brady spent the summer

Tom Brady looks for an open receiver during a preseason game against the Tampa Bay Buccaneers on August 20, 2000.

months preparing for training camp. He studied the Patriots' playbook, and worked out to add muscle to his frame. He asked questions of the veteran players and staff. By the time the preseason rolled around, Brady was ready to play.

"His attitude, after he was drafted," Brady's dad later remarked, "was that the Patriots were lucky to get him at that point in the draft. His method is that he may not be the best, but he'll outwork everyone else."[5]

As the fourth-stringer behind Bledsoe, Bishop, and Friesz, Brady played in only one game that season—a Thanksgiving Day loss to the Detroit Lions. After two interceptions by Bledsoe, Coach Belichick called on his sixth-round draft pick, who had been added to the active roster only one week prior. Brady stepped in and completed a 6-yard pass to J.R. Redmond, but received little recognition from the press for his efforts. Most fans did not even know who he was.

Despite the presence of Bledsoe and a few other key players, the Patriots had a difficult season. While the Pats had one of the league's top quarterbacks in Bledsoe, the team struggled with key plays. The Patriots finished the season with a dismal record of 5–11.

Brady, meanwhile, continued his weight training, and by the 2001 preseason had added 30 pounds of muscle to his frame. In training camp, he led all of the Patriots quarterbacks by completing 30 of 53 passes for 375 yards and 2 touchdowns, with no interceptions. Coach Belichick was impressed. "There isn't anyone on our team who works harder than Tom, in the weight room, on the field, or in the classroom," Belichick later recalled.[6]

Both Belichick and Charlie Weis, the team's offensive coordinator, were impressed at how much Brady had improved.

"There's a reason why a guy drops to the sixth round, but there's also a reason why a guy flourishes once he gets in here," Weis recalled. "He had that special moxie that it takes to be a winning quarterback. He had it at Michigan. He has it now. What he was lacking was a little bit of physical development, which he obviously has worked so diligently on to improve. The kid came in here about 180 pounds. Now he's 220 pounds. That's 40 pounds, and his body fat is still about 6 percent."[7]

That year, Belichick decided to elevate Brady to the position of backup quarterback. The Patriots coaching staff also made some changes during the off-season, gaining Antowain Smith, David Patten,

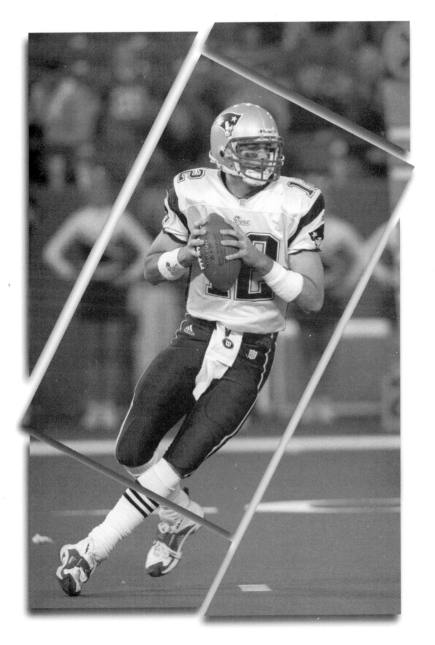

Brady scrambles outside the pocket during the Patriots' Thanksgiving Day game against the Lions in Detroit on November 23, 2000.

and Matt Light via trades. Nevertheless, the team seemed destined to have another losing season. Sportswriters predicted that the team would finish last in their division. When the Pats began the 2001 season with a 23–17 loss to Cincinnati, those predictions appeared to be coming true.

TEAM CAPTAIN

The September 23, 2001, face-off between the Patriots and the New York Jets began with emotion. Just 12 days after the September 11 terrorist attacks on the United States, the players and crowd took part in a pregame anthem to honor the victims of the horrible tragedy. In fact, many of the Jets players and staff had lost friends in the New York attacks.

Despite the somber mood, the Jets were hungry for victory. After Adam Vinatieri scored a 23-yard field goal for the Patriots in the first quarter, the Jets took command, forcing four turnovers. With just over five minutes left in the game, Drew Bledsoe scrambled to the right while running for 8 yards.

It was then that Bledsoe took a huge hit in the chest by Jets linebacker Mo Lewis. Shaken, Bledsoe returned briefly to the game before Coach Belichick pulled him out.

"The last drive that Bledsoe got hit he kind of got his bell rung," Belichick later said. "He said he was OK, I thought he was OK, but he really wasn't. I shouldn't have put him back in there."[1]

Brady stepped in to replace Bledsoe, and, in a series of passes, nearly drove the team into the end zone. While the Patriots ultimately lost 10–3, Brady played well in this tough situation.

> **Brady stepped in to replace Bledsoe, and . . . nearly drove the team into the end zone.**

That evening, Drew Bledsoe was taken to Massachusetts General Hospital, where it was determined that he was more seriously injured than he appeared. Bledsoe was suffering from internal bleeding caused by a severed blood vessel in his chest. Without immediate medical intervention, he could have died.

Brady visited Bledsoe in the hospital every day. "Drew is such a fighter," said Brady. "He got hit as hard as anyone I've ever seen."[2]

With Bledsoe out of commission for at least two weeks, Brady became the Patriots' starter. He quickly proved his skills as the Patriots faced the Indianapolis Colts, finishing 13 of 23 passes for 168 yards and leading the team to their first win of the season, 44–13. Bledsoe became a mentor to Brady, advising the younger player from the sidelines.

"Drew said the most important thing was to go out there and have fun, because you're as prepared as you're going to be at that point," Brady recalled. "This was just a good start."[3]

The following week, the Patriots played the Miami Dolphins. While Brady played fairly well, the Patriots lost 30–10. Brady took this loss to heart. He felt that the team could have played much better. "If you practice great on Wednesday and Thursday, there's no reason not to play great on Sunday," Brady said. "We need to start getting things done [during practice] every day so there's no reason to come out and play like we did today."[4]

The Patriots rebounded the following week, besting the San Diego Chargers in overtime, 29–26. Brady picked up an interior blitz and connected with receiver David Patten in overtime, setting up the game-winning goal for Vinatieri. In all, Brady completed 33 of 54 passes for 364 yards and 2 touchdowns. "It shows the type of character the guy has," Patten later said of Brady. "With the game on the line

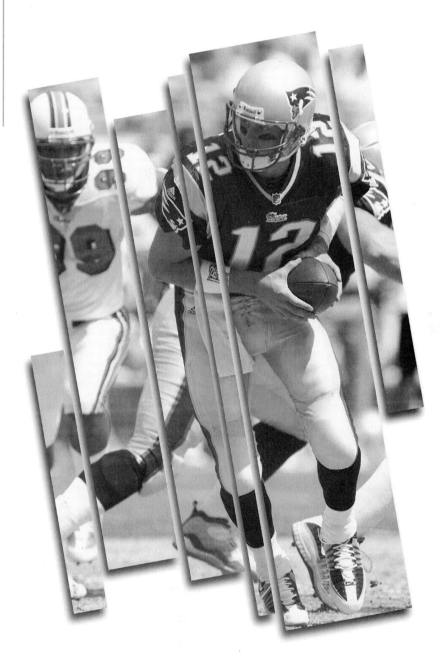

Brady is about to hand off to his running back during a game against the Miami Dolphins' at Pro Player Stadium in Miami on October 7, 2001.

like that, it just shows he's out there to make it happen."[5] For his efforts, Brady was named NFL "Player of the Week."

When Brady led the Patriots to a 38–17 victory over Indianapolis the following week, fans and reporters began to take notice of the young quarterback. The Patriots were now 3–1 with Brady starting. Newspaper reporters questioned what would happen when Drew Bledsoe was cleared to play. Bledsoe had been the cornerstone of the Patriots, yet the team was winning with Brady on the field. Brady chose to stay focused on his game rather than speculating on the situation.

The Pats lost their next game to the Denver Broncos, led by Brady's former Michigan rival, Brian Griese. Brady was critical of his own plays in the 31–20 loss. "You can't miss throws like I did out there," he later said. "I'd been making those throws before. I've got to do a better job of communicating with the receivers. I'm the checks and balances guy out there, so when there is a mix-up it's my fault."[6]

Brady realized, though, that he could not dwell on such mistakes. There were more games to be played. "There's been hard times before that I've had," he said. "You learn how to deal with them and just move forward."[7] New England rebounded with victories in their next two games, versus the Atlanta Falcons and the Buffalo Bills. Brady received some criticism for his performance in this game, in which he was sacked 7 times and made 2 fumbles. Newspaper reporters commented that Brady was "finally playing like a rookie."[8]

Brady did not let the criticism interrupt his focus. He was put to the test when the Pats played the St. Louis Rams, one of the toughest teams in the NFL. Although the Pats ended up losing 24–17, Brady felt that the team performed well against such a powerful opponent. "We played against a real good team and were right there with them," Brady said. "People can say whatever they want about the New England Patriots, but this defense is good enough to keep us in every game."[9]

Following this loss to the Rams, the Patriots defeated the New Orleans Saints, thanks in part to four touchdown passes by Brady. The following week, the Patriots came back from a 13-point deficit to overcome the Jets, 17–16. Although Drew Bledsoe was cleared to play in this game, Coach Belichick opted to stick with Brady. Bledsoe was disappointed. Reporters compared the two quarterbacks, and reportedly questioned Brady about the Bledsoe

Brady calls the play from behind center during a game against the Buffalo Bills in Foxboro, Massachusetts, on November 11, 2001.

situation. Brady dismissed the rumors by expressing his admiration for Bledsoe.

Nearing the end of the regular season, Brady led the Patriots to victories over the Cleveland Browns, Buffalo Bills, and Miami Dolphins. He became the only quarterback in Patriots history to win 11 of his first 14 starts. With a 38–6 victory over the Carolina Panthers, the Patriots were headed for the playoffs. Fans and reporters were stunned. The 5–11 team of one season ago had now become a serious contender.

The Patriots began the AFC Divisional Playoffs with a game against the Oakland Raiders on a snowy day at Foxboro stadium. With the Raiders leading 7–0 at halftime, it appeared as if the Patriots were destined for a loss. In the second half, however, Adam Vinatieri made a field goal to bring the Pats onto the scoreboard, 7–3. Oakland fought back with two field goals, extending their lead to 10 by the end of the third quarter.

Heading into the fourth quarter, Brady stepped up the pace, completing nine straight passes before running for a touchdown on a quarterback draw. With the score now at 13–10 and 1:50 left in the game, Oakland's cornerback Charles Woodson blitzed and hit Brady for an apparent fumble that was recovered by Oakland to end the threat.

Brady scrambles through the snow during the playoff game against the Oakland Raiders played on January 19, 2002.

With 1:43 remaining, linebacker Greg Biekert of the Raiders had recovered the ball and the play was ruled a fumble. It appeared as if the Patriots had lost the game.

Soon, however, a call came that the play was being reviewed by officials. After reviewing the play, referee Walt Coleman announced that Brady's apparent "fumble" was in fact being ruled an incomplete pass under what was called the "tuck rule." That rule stated that once a player clearly indicates a pass, any arm movement forward will denote a pass unless he tucks the ball under his arm. Since Brady's arm had been moving the ball forward to steady it with his other hand when he was tackled, the play was designated a pass.

This ruling gave the Patriots the opportunity to tie the game—and Brady's record clearly showed that the young quarterback would make it happen. With Oakland and New England fans watching in awe, Brady led a drive to set up the game-tying field goal for Adam Vinatieri. The field goal, completed by Vinatieri, brought the game into overtime, and the Patriots won, 16–13.

Oakland players and fans alike were upset about the ruling that ultimately lost them the game. Walt Coleman later explained, "When I got over to the replay monitor and looked it was obvious that his arm was coming forward, he was trying to tuck the ball and they just knocked it out of his hand. His hand was coming forward, which makes it an incomplete pass."[10]

Although many in Oakland did not agree with the end result, most could not help but be impressed with Brady's heroics throughout the game. In all, Brady completed 26 of 39 passes in the second half alone. "Watching him, you'd think he had 10 years in this league," Vinatieri said of Brady. "He just has so much poise."[11]

Following that win, the Pats went on to face the Pittsburgh Steelers for the AFC Championship and the chance to play at the Super Bowl. Leading in the second quarter, Brady sprained his ankle and was forced to leave the game. Drew Bledsoe stepped in and connected with David Patten for a touchdown. Bledsoe and the Pats held onto their lead, ultimately winning the game, 24–17. The underdog Patriots had clinched the AFC Championship and would be headed to the Super Bowl. Brady was ecstatic.

> **"He just has so much poise."**
>
> **—Adam Vinatieri**

For the Patriots, it would not be an easy game. They would play the strongest team in the NFL, the St. Louis Rams. The media set up a "David and Goliath" showdown for the two teams. Most felt that the Patriots had been lucky thus far, and would not be able to keep up with the Rams.

Coach Belichick now had an important decision to make. He would have to choose his starting quarterback. Many longtime Patriots fans felt that Drew Bledsoe, as the veteran player, should be given the starting position. But the chemistry of the team seemed to be better with Brady as the quarterback.

Brady hands off during the AFC Championship game played against the Pittsburgh Steelers at Heinz Field in Pittsburgh, Pennsylvania, on January 27, 2002.

Reporters and fans waited excitedly for Coach Belichick's decision.

For the veteran coach, it really was not a tough decision at all. Brady, who had led the team this far, would be the starter. Brady would be the third-youngest quarterback (behind Dan Marino and David Woodley) to start in a Super Bowl.

Brady's teammates approved of the coach's selection. They had faith in Brady as their leader. Drew Bledsoe was disappointed, but handled the situation with dignity, cheering for Brady and supporting the coach's decision. "This is the biggest game there is," he said.[12]

Brady was now the center of a media frenzy. Everyone wanted to know more about him. People stopped him for autographs. Reporters hounded him for interviews. Brady, however, chose to think of the Super Bowl as "just another game." He was confident that the Patriots could overcome the Rams.

"The great thing about Tom," said Rams quarterback Kurt Warner, "is that no matter what he went through, it didn't seem like he allowed the pressure to bother him."[13]

The Pats were inspired by their leader's calm, self-assured demeanor.

In fact, Brady was so confident in his team that he decided to relax in the locker room before the game. Soon, he fell asleep on the floor. He woke up refreshed, relaxed, and hungry for victory. Tom Brady was about to make history.

7

MVP

The Patriots' Super Bowl victory made Tom Brady a household name. As MVP, Brady was presented with a trophy and a brand new Cadillac SUV. The media reported that the truck's sticker price was more than Brady's entire signing bonus with the Patriots.

"As far as I'm concerned," Brady said, "the emotional ride has been straight up. There hasn't been a downer yet, except this morning at about 6:00 A.M. when the alarm went off. Other than that, it's been pretty awesome."[1]

Following the Super Bowl, Brady headed to Hawaii to take part in the Pro Bowl. He became only the fifth quarterback since 1970 to earn a trip to the Pro Bowl in his first year as a starter. Several terminally ill children from the "Make A Wish" foundation were present at the Pro Bowl. Brady spent much of his time talking with and signing autographs for the children. According to Dave Reardon of the *Boston Herald*, "Brady didn't just scribble his name and run away. He chatted with them for a good 10 minutes. He learned their names, their favorite foods, whom else they had met . . . ."[2]

By this time, Brady's life had become a whirlwind of public appearances. Along with the entire team, Brady was invited to the White House as a special guest of President Bush. He appeared in a Disney World parade, judged the Miss USA beauty pageant, and appeared in a "Got Milk" commercial. Brady was featured on the covers of several magazines, and was named one of *People* magazine's "50 Most Beautiful People."

As he grew more popular, however, Brady found that his life was changing. He could no longer take everyday tasks for granted. Whenever he went out in public, he was mobbed by fans. He could no longer eat dinner at his favorite restaurants, or play baseball near Foxboro Stadium. Adoring female fans sent marriage proposals and left gifts and flowers at his doorstep. Teenaged girls invited him to their school proms. Although Brady was grateful to fans for their support, he found the lack of privacy to be difficult. He made sure that he did not lose sight of what is truly important in life.

"All of this attention is flattering," Brady later said, "But that's not what gives me peace of mind. What truly makes me happy is hanging with my parents, my family and my friends."[3]

Brady was grateful to his family and friends for supporting him through the years. He presented his Super Bowl ring to his dad, with thanks for his love and support.

> "What truly makes me happy is hanging with my parents, my family and my friends."
>
> —Tom Brady

During the off-season, the Patriots made several key changes to the team. Christian Fauria, Cam Cleeland, and Deion Branch were added to the Patriots' roster. In April 2002, Drew Bledsoe was traded to the Buffalo Bills, leaving no doubt that Brady would remain the team's leader. In August, the Pats signed Brady to a four-year contract.

As the defending Super Bowl champions, the 2002–03 season would be a tough one for the Patriots. The Pats began the season strong, winning their first

Brady looks to pass during a game against the Chicago Bears on November 10, 2002.

three games. But the constant media attention interrupted the team's focus. Soon, the team began to struggle, losing their next four games. Reporters questioned whether the Super Bowl win had been a fluke.

"We just had a bad stretch in the middle of the year and it cost us," Brady said. "We played four teams, lost four in a row, and then it was a struggle to get back to a winning record by the end of the year. I think that was a time where there was some serious evaluation that went on, from being 3–0 to 3–4, and then saying where do we go from here? You know we fought back, but it just wasn't enough."[4]

As the quarterback and team leader, Brady received criticism for the losses. He did not make excuses, but promised to work harder.

"Why do some guys have one great year and then play so badly the next? Well, now I think I know why—because there are so many things that can take you away from what you need to do to focus on your job. My biggest fear is to end up being a one-hit wonder."[5]

In the final game of the regular season, Brady led the Patriots to a 27–24 overtime victory over the Miami Dolphins. But the competition was

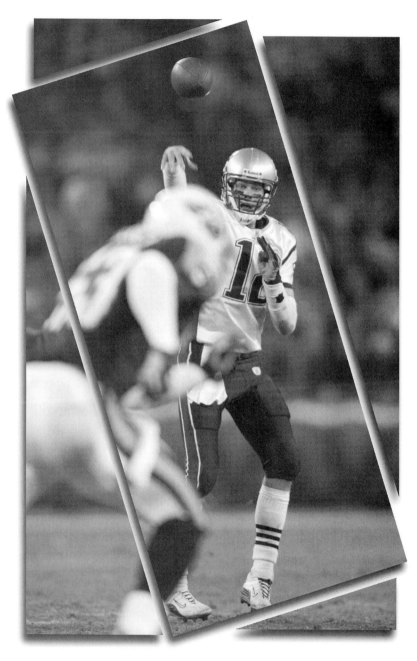

Tom Brady tries to connect with one of his receivers during a
game against the Tennessee Titans on December 16, 2002.

particularly tough that year, and the Pats failed to make the playoffs.

Although it was not a particularly good season for the Pats, Brady's individual statistics were impressive. He completed the season with 3,763 yards, 28 touchdowns, and connections on more than 60% of his passes. Nevertheless, Brady was disappointed in the team's—and his own—performance.

"One thing I've learned," he later said, "is I have to find time for myself. The other thing is you have to make sure you are able to prepare to play football. You can't let anything else get in the way of that."[6]

During the off-season, Brady underwent surgery for a separated shoulder that had occurred during the final game with Miami. As soon as he was able, Brady was back to lifting weights and working out. By the start of the 2003 season, Brady was ready to return to his winning form.

"[The offseason] has been good," Brady said. "I feel a bit more refreshed and we have a little more time to get focused on winning some football games."[7]

8

A STELLAR SEASON

The 2003 season began with a meeting between the Patriots and the Buffalo Bills. The media created a showdown between Brady and Drew Bledsoe, now the Bills' starting quarterback. It was also the teams' first meeting since veteran Lawyer Milloy had been traded to the Bills.

From the beginning, Buffalo appeared to have the upper hand. Brady's game was shaky, and he threw 4 interceptions. In the second quarter, Buffalo's Sam Adams picked off a pass by Brady and scored a touchdown. The Patriots remained scoreless throughout the game. For the first time in ten years, the Patriots were shut out, with an embarrassing final score of 31–0.

Brady rebounded in the next game, in which the Pats played the Philadelphia Eagles. He passed for 255 yards and 3 touchdowns to lead the Patriots past the Eagles, 31–10. Brady and the Patriots then topped the New York Jets 23–16, despite the injuries of four starters. After tumbling 20–17 to the Washington Redskins, the Patriots scored victories over Tennessee and the New York Giants. Brady then led the Patriots to a 19–13 victory in overtime over the Miami Dolphins, with an 82-yard touchdown pass to Troy Brown. It was the first time in fifteen games that the Patriots defeated Miami on the road.

After conquering the Cleveland Browns, 9–3, the Patriots topped Denver, 30–26. Brady tossed an 18-yard touchdown pass to David Givens with 30 seconds left to play. The Pats then earned their first shutout in seven seasons, with a 12–0 defeat of the Dallas Cowboys, headed by former New England coach, Bill Parcells.

By this time, the Patriots were clearly on a winning streak. Victories over Houston and Indianapolis followed. In blizzard conditions on December 7 at Foxboro, the Patriots shut out Miami, 12–0; Brady was 16 for 31 for 163 yards. The Pats became the first team in the NFL to clinch their division.

In yet another snow-covered game, the Pats

Tom Brady is embraced by former teammate Drew Bledsoe (right) after a game between Brady's Patriots and Bledsoe's Buffalo Bills in 2003.

trumped Jacksonville, 27–13. The Patriots continued their winning streak with a 21–16 victory over the New York Jets. They followed with their third shutout of the season—a 31–0 victory over the Buffalo Bills. The Pats had accomplished the longest NFL winning streak since the Miami Dolphins in 1983–84. With this winning record, the Pats were guaranteed "home field advantage" in the playoffs.

Brady's performance during the regular season was equally impressive. His 34–12 career record thus far gave him a .739 winning percentage, higher than any other active quarterback with 25 or more starts. Brady attributed much of this success to his teammates.

"Over the course of the last 14 games," Brady said, "we developed something special. It's a mental toughness, a sense of complete preparation, and we feel we can overcome any obstacle."[1]

Despite the Patriots' terrific season and winning percentage, Brady was not selected to play in the Pro Bowl. He ranked 10th overall among starting quarterbacks in Pro Bowl standings. However, Brady placed third in the NFL regular season MVP balloting, behind Steve McNair of Tennessee and Peyton Manning of Indianapolis, who shared MVP honors.

Brady would face both McNair and Manning once the playoffs began. The Pats took on McNair and Tennessee in the divisional playoffs on January 10. The weather in Foxboro at game time was 11 degrees below zero. Despite the bitter cold, fans packed into Gillette Stadium to watch the Pats trounce the Titans, 17–14. The Pats were about to advance to their second AFC title game in three seasons.

Following this victory, Brady attended the State of the Union Address in Washington, D.C. as a guest of President and Mrs. Bush. Then it was back to Foxboro to prepare for the AFC Championship game,

Tom Brady celebrates his team's victory over the Tennessee Titans on October 5, 2003. The game would mark the beginning of what would eventually become an NFL-record winning streak.

where the Patriots would face Peyton Manning and the Indianapolis Colts.

The January 18 AFC title game took place on another snowy day. The game was an exciting one, as the Pats defeated the Colts, 24–14. Adam Vinatieri made 5 field goals to secure the win for the Pats. The Patriots overpowered Manning, as the MVP threw 4 interceptions and was sacked 4 times. The crowd went wild—the Pats were headed to the Super Bowl in Houston, Texas!

Unlike two years prior, the Patriots were now the Super Bowl favorites. The Pats would play the Carolina Panthers, led by quarterback Jake Delhomme. An undrafted free agent, Delhomme had been invited to the New Orleans Saints' camp in 1997. He was waived three times by the Saints, before the Panthers picked him up in March 2003. Delhomme had thrown only 10 passes in the previous three years.

While Delhomme was several years older than Brady, he looked up to the younger quarterback. In an interview prior to the Super Bowl, Delhomme commented that Brady was his "professional role model." While Brady was flattered, he remained humble. Brady joked to the press, "You mean he wants to be slow with an average arm?"[2] Despite all that he had accomplished thus far, Brady still could

Peyton Manning (left) of the Indianapolis Colts congratulates Tom Brady after the Patriots defeated the Colts in the AFC Championship Game on January 18, 2004.

not believe that he had achieved such superstar status.

As the Pats prepared for their second Super Bowl in three years, Brady was compared to his childhood idol, Joe Montana. Brady felt that such a comparison was premature. "I think that's crazy," he said. "Joe was the best quarterback in the history of the NFL. I think it's flattering, but it's pretty unrealistic. I would love to have some of the traits that Joe possessed, but there's a long way to go."[3]

Charlie Weis, the Patriots offensive coordinator,

could see why Brady was compared with the great Montana. "We talk about the word 'it.' He has it," Weis told the press. "I can't define the word 'it,' but certain quarterbacks have it and certain quarterbacks don't. Tom Brady is the epitome of having that special it."[4]

9

ON TOP OF THE WORLD

Sportswriters had predicted that Super Bowl XXXVIII would be won on defense. For a while, that appeared to be the case. After a scoreless first quarter, Panthers quarterback Jake Delhomme had completed only one of six passes, for a total of one yard. Carolina had –7 net yards of total offense after the game's first 20 plays. The Patriots' strong defense had been able to keep the Panthers at bay.

But Carolina was not an easy opponent, keeping the Patriots scoreless as well. Midway through the second quarter, the score remained 0–0. Then, with just three minutes remaining before halftime, Brady completed a 5-yard touchdown pass to Deion Branch to bring the Patriots up, 7–0. It was the latest initial score in the history of the Super Bowl.

The Panthers were ready to fight back. Delhomme scrambled, tossing a huge pass down the left side to Carolina's Steve Smith. The game was tied at 7–7.

Brady brought the Patriots back up, 14–7, with a 5-yard touchdown pass to David Givens. The Panthers' John Kasay then kicked a 50-yard field goal to end the first half at 14–10. In the last three minutes before halftime, the teams had scored a combined 24 points.

The Pats dominated in the third quarter, but did not reach scoring position until the fourth. Brady threw for 16 yards to Deion Branch. Antowain Smith ran twice for 10 yards, and Branch made a catch for another 8. Brady then made a huge throw down the middle to Daniel Graham for a gain of 33 yards.

"Tom is the kind of guy who believes in everybody who's on the field playing with him. Doesn't matter who's out there with him. He has total confidence that that person will go out there and do their job," teammate Damien Woody said. "When you have a quarterback like that out there on the field, it makes everybody's job out there a lot easier knowing that, 'Hey, he's got my back. I'm going to go out there and play that much harder for a guy who believes in me.'"[1]

A touchdown by Smith brought the score to 21–10, Patriots. But it was not over yet. There was still 14:49 left to play.

Jake Delhomme rose to the occasion, throwing to Muhsin Muhammed for 13 yards. The Panthers' DeShaun Foster answered with a 33-yard touchdown run. Carolina Coach John Fox went for a two-point conversion, which the Panthers missed.

Brady, with a chance to finish off the opponent, made an uncharacteristic mistake. On the Pats 27-yard line, he underthrew toward tight-end Christian Fauria. The ball was caught by Carolina's Reggie Howard in the end zone. Howard picked the ball and carried it to his own 10-yard line. The Panthers now had a chance to take the lead.

"I didn't make the best throw," Brady recalled. "I was throwing to the right guy, but I didn't put enough air under it."[2]

Delhomme took full advantage of the situation, tossing an 85-yard touchdown pass to Muhsin Muhammed, the longest play from scrimmage in Super Bowl history. The Panthers took a 22–21 lead,

Tom Brady is caught from behind by Carolina Panthers safety Mike Minter during the second quarter of Super Bowl XXXVIII, played on February 1, 2004.

with 6:53 left to play. It was the first time the Pats had trailed in a game since November 23.

Brady was not about to let the one mistake get the best of him. He stayed calm, driving the ball to the Panthers' 3-yard line with a series of passes to David Givens. Brady then reached Mike Vrabel with a touchdown pass. The Patriots led by a touchdown.

"[Brady] is one of the main reasons why everyone else stays calm in tight situations," said teammate Deion Branch.[3]

With 2:51 left, the Panthers needed a touchdown to tie the game. Delhomme rallied, moving his team into Patriots' territory and reaching Muhammad for 19 yards. Delhomme then lofted a pass to Ricky Proehl with 1:08 left, to tie the score at 29. But the Panthers' John Kasay, on his kickoff, sent the ball out of bounds. The Pats would take over at their own 40.

With 1:08 remaining, Brady could think of nothing but winning the game. "There's a confidence that we can do anything," he later said.[4]

Brady threw to Troy Brown for a first down. But offensive pass interference was called against the Patriots, sending the team back 10 yards. Brady tossed to Brown for 13 and followed with a pass to Graham for 4. On third-and-three, Brady threw to Deion Branch on the right side for 17 yards and Branch made his tenth catch of the game at the Panthers' 23-yard line.

> **"Tom is at his best in those two-minute situations."**
>
> —Bill Belichick

As it had in 2001, the final minute of the Super Bowl came down to Brady and Adam Vinatieri.

"Tom is at his best in those two-minute situations," Bill Belichick later said. "Or one, as the case may be."[5]

With nine seconds left, Vinatieri prepared to make the 41-yard attempt. A hush came over the crowd at Houston. Vinatieri had missed two field goals earlier in the game—would he make this one? Few could forget that the kicker had made a 48-yard goal in 2001, when the Patriots defeated the Rams.

As the crowd held its breath, Vinatieri made the kick. It was good. New England had won, 32–29. The Pats had won their second Super Bowl in just three years. The crowd leapt to its feet. Confetti poured onto the field, covering the players.

Brady's teammates could not say enough about their captain.

"Brady, man I can't say enough about that guy," said Antowain Smith. "He marched us down the field and put us in position for the winning kick."[6]

"To win this, the way we did it, is just incredible. Just a great, all-around game," Brady said. "You don't dream of winning Super Bowls like this. The way it ended was just incredible."[7]

The fourth-quarter point total of 37 was noted as the highest-scoring period ever in a Super Bowl. In that period alone, Brady was 13-for-19 for 136 yards. Both Brady and Delhomme had passed for at least 300 yards, making it only the second time in Super Bowl history that both quarterbacks achieved such a feat. Brady also made 32 pass completions, surpassing the record of 31 that Jim Kelly had set in Super Bowl XXVIII.

Tom Brady holds the Vince Lombardi trophy after the Patriots'
victory over the Carolina Panthers in Super Bowl XXXVIII on
February 1, 2004.

There was little question as to who was the star of the game. For the second time in three years, Tom Brady was named Super Bowl MVP. As a two-time winner, he joined the ranks of Joe Montana, Bart Starr, and Terry Bradshaw.

"Tom Brady is the greatest winner in football right now," said teammate Ty Law. "Maybe his numbers are not eye-popping, all these yards, all these touchdowns. But he knows how to win."[8]

"Tom's going to be mentioned with the better quarterbacks playing now and in the past," Patriots coach Bill Belichick said. "You can't deny his production. He's a winner. He does what he needs to do to help the team win, and he does it as well as anybody."[9]

Brady celebrated the Super Bowl victory with his teammates before flying to Disney World for a parade. An exhausted Brady then was back in Boston for the Patriots' hometown celebration, before heading off to California for the Pebble Beach Pro-Am Golf Tournament.

To many, Brady is living a fairytale life. He is young, handsome, and successful, with two Super Bowl rings and just as many game MVP trophies. But Brady is not the type to rest on his laurels.

"Yesterday, for as great as it was, it really wasn't

Tom Brady is sacked during a Halloween game against the Steelers in Pittsburgh in 2004. Pittsburgh's victory in the game snapped the Pats' record 21-game winning streak (18 games in the regular season).

perfect," Brady said after the Super Bowl. "So there's always things to improve on, still a lot of room to grow."[10]

Brady and the Patriots kept right on rolling as they entered the 2004 season. They won their first six games to extend their record winning streak to 18 straight games (21 counting the postseason). The Pittsburgh Steelers broke the streak in week eight, but the Pats would avenge that loss by beating the

Steelers in the AFC Championship game. Two weeks later, on February 6, 2005, they defeated the Philadelphia Eagles to win their third Super Bowl in four years. Tom Brady had helped establish a new football dynasty in New England.

Brady has many more successful years ahead of him. His teammates look forward to working with him. He stepped in when called, and became the leader that the Patriots needed.

Tom Brady may not be the league's best passer or have the greatest footwork. He does not have the strongest arm, and will never be the NFL's strongest player. But Tom Brady knows how to win games, and he knows how to lead his team. And above all, Tom Brady has the heart of a champion.

As teammate Christian Fauria once said, "Above any way he throws the ball, [Brady's] biggest asset is he knows how to lead men. If he was in the Army, he'd be a general. He'd be the guy leading the troops, but he wouldn't just lead them, he'd be on the front lines with them. He'd go fight himself and be in front of everybody."[11]

CHAPTER
NOTES

Chapter I. Making History

1. "NFL.com wire report," *NFL.com*, February 3, 2002, <http://www.nfl.com> (August 20, 2004).

2. Ibid.

3. Andrew Mason, "Pats bring new meaning to 'team,'" *NFL.com*, February 3, 2002, <http://www.nfl.com> (August 20, 2004).

4. *New England Sportsline*, February 2002, <http://newenglandsportsline.com/champs/pats-xxxvi-tomb.html> (August 20, 2004).

5. "NFL.com wire report," February 3, 2002.

6. Tim Polzer, "No Midnight for Cinderella MVP Brady," February 3, 2002, <http://www.superbowl.com/> (August 20, 2004).

7. Bob Ryan, "Brady Tops Off Tale for the Ages," *Boston Globe Online*, February 4, 2002, <http://www.bostonglobe.com> (August 20, 2004).

8. Tim Polzer, "No Midnight for Cinderella MVP Brady."

9. Ibid.

10. Ibid.

11. Ibid.

Chapter 2. Early Years

1. "NFL's Under the Helmet: Back in the Day with Tom Brady," November 27, 2002, <http:www.nfl.com/reebok/bid/tbrady.html> (August 20, 2004).

2. Ibid.

3. Ibid.

4. Greg Garber, "Brady Following in Steps of His Idol," *ESPN.com*, January 27, 2004, <http://sports.espn.go.com/nfl/playoffs03/columns/story?columnist=garber_greg&id=1719979> (August 20, 2004).

5. Ibid.

6. "NFL's Under the Helmet: Back in the Day with Tom Brady."

7. Ibid.

8. Troy Gunderson, "New England Patriots Quarterback has Family Ties to Central Minnesota." *Brainerd Dispatch*, <http://www.absolutebrady.com/Articles/BIOCont.html> (August 20, 2004).

9. "NFL's Under the Helmet: Back in the Day with Tom Brady."

10. Sharon Chin, "San Mateo Cheers Hometown MVP," *Kpix*, February 4, 2002, <http://beta.kpix.com/news/local/2002/02/04/San_Mateo_Cheers_Hometown_MVP.html> (August 20, 2004).

11. "Up for the challenge: The Tougher the Test, the Better Patriots' QB Brady Likes It," *New York Times*, February 3, 2002, <http://www.absolutebrady.com/Archive/January2004.html> (August 20, 2004).

12. Gunderson.

13. Ron Kroichick, "Bradys Are Family Affair," *SF Gate*, January 18, 2002, <http://www.absolutebrady.com/Articles/BIOSFGate011802.html> (August 20, 2004).

Chapter 3. Young All-Star

1. George Devine, Sr., "Super Bowl Hero—Serra High's Tom Brady: Team Player with Work Ethic," March 22, 2002, <http://www.absolutebrady.com> (August 20, 2004).

2. "NFL's Under the Helmet: Back in the Day with Tom Brady," November 27, 2002, <http:www.nfl. com/reebok/bid/tbrady.html> (August 20, 2004).

3. Devine.

4. "NFL's Under the Helmet: Back in the Day with Tom Brady."

5. Ibid.

6. Devine.

7. "NFL's Under the Helmet: Back in the Day with Tom Brady."

8. Mark Murphy, "From Big Blue to Replacing Drew," *Boston Herald*, September 30, 2001, in *Tom Brady: Most Valuable Patriot* (Boston Herald/Sports Publishing, 2002), pp. 20–26.

Chapter 4. Michigan Days

1. Mark Murphy, "From Big Blue to Replacing Drew," Boston Herald, September 30, 2001, in *Tom Brady: Most Valuable Patriot* (Boston Herald/Sports Publishing, 2002), pp. 20–26.

2. "Squeezing Out a Victory," *CNN/SI*, January 9, 1999, <http://sportsillustrated.cnn.com/football/ college/1998/bowls/citrus/> (August 20, 2004).

3. Mark Maske, "Brady's Rise to 'King of the Hill,'" *Washington Post*, January 28, 2004, p. D04.

4. Ibid.

5. Ibid.

6. Lenny Megliola, "Brady-Henson Pair Was a Gem," *Metrowest News*, January 27, 2004, <http://www. metrowestdailynews.com/sports/columnists/ scolreiss01272004.htm> (August 20, 2004).

7. Mark Murphy, "From Big Blue to Replacing Drew."

8. Lisa Lombardo, "Tom Brady—Absolutely," *Vteens. org*, September 11, 2002, <http://www.vteens.org/ content.cfm?fuseaction=article&article_id= 452&channel=4> (August 20, 2004).

Chapter 5. Pro Player

1. Mark Murphy, "From Big Blue to Replacing Drew." *Boston Herald*, September 30, 2001, in *Tom Brady: Most Valuable Patriot* (Boston Herald/Sports Publishing, 2002), pp. 20–26.
2. Ibid.
3. Michael Silver, "Super Bowl MVP Tom Brady—The Natural—A Whirlwind Off-Season for the New Prince of the NFL," *Sports Illustrated*, April 15, 2002, <http://www.absolutebrady.com/Articles/BIOsi041502.html> (August 20, 2004).
4. Mark Murphy, "From Big Blue to Replacing Drew."
5. Ibid.
6. Michael Silver, "American Idol." *Sports Illustrated Presents: The New England Patriots*, February 11, 2004, p. 12.
7. Mark Murphy, "From Big Blue to Replacing Drew."

Chapter 6. Team Captain

1. *Yahoo Sports Canada News Report*, September 23, 2001, <ca.sports.yahoo.com/nfl/rcps/week2/nyjnwe.html> (August 20, 2004).
2. Mark Murphy, "Backup Hears Call," *Tom Brady: Most Valuable Patriot* (Boston Herald/Sports Publishing, 2002), p. 14.
3. Mark Murphy, "Understudy Acts Like Leading Man," *Tom Brady: Most Valuable Patriot* (Boston Herald/Sports Publishing, 2002), p. 28.
4. Kevin Mannix, "Following Milloy's Lead," *Tom Brady: Most Valuable Patriot* (Boston Herald/Sports Publishing, 2002), p. 36.
5. Michael Felger, "Brady in Control," *Tom Brady: Most Valuable Patriot* (Boston Herald/Sports Publishing, 2002), p. 43.
6. Kevin Mannix, "Facing a Crucial Test," *Tom Brady:*

Most Valuable Patriot (Boston Herald/Sports Publishing, 2002), p. 50.

7. Karen Guregian, "Rebounding from Denver," *Tom Brady: Most Valuable Patriot* (Boston Herald/Sports Publishing, 2002), p. 53.

8. Kevin Mannix, "Finally Playing Like a Rookie," *Tom Brady: Most Valuable Patriot* (Boston Herald/Sports Publishing, 2002), p. 72.

9. Ibid.

10. Peter Lawrence-Riddell, "Controversy Thrives in Patriots-Raiders Encounters," *ESPN.com*, January 19, 2002, <http://espn.go.com/nfl/playoffs01/s/2002/0119/1314426.html> (August 20, 2004).

11. Karen Guregian, "A Star is Born—Again," *Tom Brady: Most Valuable Patriot* (Boston Herald/Sports Publishing, 2002), p. 99.

12. Kevin Mannix, "Still the Man," *Tom Brady: Most Valuable Patriot* (Boston Herald/Sports Publishing, 2002), p. 105.

13. Michael Silver, "American Idol." *Sports Illustrated Presents: The New England Patriots*, February 11, 2004, p. 12.

Chapter 7. MVP

1. George Kimball, "Rewards Come by Truckload for MVP," *Tom Brady: Most Valuable Patriot* (Boston Herald/Sports Publishing, 2002), p. 108.

2. Dave Reardon, "Kid Stuff not a Passing Concern," *Tom Brady: Most Valuable Patriot* (Boston Herald/Sports Publishing, 2002), p. 114.

3. Michael Silver, "American Idol," *Sports Illustrated Presents: The New England Patriots*, February 11, 2004, p. 12.

4. Paul Perillo, "No Nonsense Brady on Display," *Boston Herald*, July 1, 2003, p. B1.

5. Michael Silver, "American Idol."

6. Jackie MacMullen, "No Avoiding This Rush," *Boston Globe*, February 1, 2004, p. B1.

7. Paul Perillo, "No Nonsense Brady."

Chapter 8. A Stellar Season

1. Michael Silver, "All Systems Go," *Sports Illustrated Presents: New England Patriots*, February 11, 2004, p. 48.

2. Mike Lowe, "Ho-Hum, All He Does Is Win," *Portland Press Herald*, January 25, 2004, <http://sports.mainetoday.com/pro/patriots/040125brady.shtml> (August 20, 2004).

3. Bernie Miklasz, "Brady Wants to Be More than Just an Average Joe," *STL Today*, January 29, 2004, <http://www.stltoday.com/stltoday/sports/columnists.nsf/Bernie+Miklasz/440885A7D9C132FA86256E2B001A3EC2?opendocument&Headline=Brady+wants+to+be+more+than+just+an+average+Joe> (August 20, 2004).

4. Murphy, "From Big Blue to Replacing Drew," *Boston Herald*, September 30, 2001, in *Tom Brady: Most Valuable Patriot* (Boston Herald/Sports Publishing, 2002), pp. 20–26.

Chapter 9. On Top of the World

1. Jon Couture, "Eyes on the Prize: Tom Brady Has Come a Long Way," *South Coast Standard Times*, January 3, 2004, p. B1.

2. Dave Boling, "A Very Brady Sequel to Joe Montana?" *News Tribune*, February 2, 2004, <http://www.tribnet.com/sports/columnists/dave_boling/story/4697412p-4648654c.html>.

3. Ibid.

4. Ibid.

5. Ibid.

6. Ibid.

7. Michael Silver, "What a Finish," *Sports Illustrated Presents: New England Patriots*, February 11, 2004, p. 54.

8. Tom Pedulla, "A Very Brady Sequel," *USA Today*, January 27, 2004, p. C1.

9. Vic Carucci, "Brady Takes Place Among Game's Best," February 1, 2004, <http://www.superbowl.com/news/story/7055564> (August 20, 2004).

10. Boling.

11. Howard Ulman, "New England Patriots Quarterback Tom Brady Sharp as NFL Playoffs Start," Associated Press, January 2, 2004.

CAREER STATISTICS

Passing

Year	ATT	CMP	PCT	YDS	YDS/PASS	SK	LP	IN	TD
2000	3	1	33.3	6	2.00	0	6	0	0
2001	413	264	63.9	2,843	6.88	41	91	12	18
2002	601	373	62.1	3,764	6.26	31	49	14	28
2003	527	317	60.2	3,620	6.87	29	82	12	23
2004	474	288	60.8	3,692	7.79	26	50	14	28
Total	2,018	1,243	61.6	13,925	6.90	127	91	52	97

Postseason Passing

Year	ATT	CMP	PCT	YDS	YDS/PASS	SK	SYL	LP	IN	TD
2001	97	60	61.9	572	6	5	36	29	1	1
2003	48	32	66.7	354	7	0	0	52	1	3
2004	81	55	67.9	587	7	7	57	60	0	5
Total	226	147	65.0	1,513	7	12	93	60	2	9

ATT—Attempts
CMP—Completion
PCT—Percentage
YDS—Yards

YDS/PASS—Yards per Pass
SK—Sacks
SYL—Sack Yardage Lost

LP—Longest Passing
IN—Interception
TD—Touchdown
LRU—Longest Rushing

Rushing

Year	ATT	YDS	AVG	LRU	TD
2000	0	0	0	0	0
2001	36	43	1.2	12	0
2002	42	110	2.6	15	1
2003	42	63	1.5	11	1
2004	43	28	0.7	10	0
Total	163	244	1.5	15	2

Postseason Rushing

Year	ATT	YDS	AVG	LRU	TD
2001	8	22	2.8	6	1
2003	2	12	6.0	12	0
2004	7	3	0.4	3	1
Total	17	37	2.2	12	2

ATT—Attempts **YDS/PASS**—Yards per Pass **LP**—Longest Passing
CMP—Completion **IN**—Interception
PCT—Percentage **SK**—Sacks **TD**—Touchdown
YDS—Yards **SYL**—Sack Yardage Lost **LRU**—Longest Rushing

WHERE TO WRITE

Mr. Tom Brady
New England Patriots
Gillette Stadium
Foxboro, MA 02035

INTERNET ADDRESSES

New England Patriots: Official Site

http://www.patriots.com

Email a Patriot:

http://www.patriots.com/fanzone/public/index.
cfm?ac=playerfeedback

INDEX